But First, Can You Tie My Shoe?

Enjoy the journey of parenthood!
Jeannie O. Harsha

But First, Can You Tie My Shoe?

Jeannie O. Harsha

with contributions by
Karen Molenaar Terrell and Annie Barrett

Images and photos by the author or Xlibris except for the following:

Jill Ballinger is the photographer for "The Calm Before the Heat", "To My 15-Year Old" and "Reminder"; Jolie Harsha contributed the photo for "Head to Head at Sunrise"; author's photo by Tara Lowry.

To order additional copies of this book, contact:
Xlibris Corporation
1-888-795-4274
www.Xlibris.com
Orders@Xlibris.com
70040

CONTENTS

Book Dedication

For Jeff, my steadfast partner in this parenting adventure; and for
Jason and Jenner, my inspiration.

Acknowledgements

The thought-provoking influence of the teachers and fellow students at Emerson Institute helped launch this project. I am extremely grateful to them and others at the Positive Living Center in Oakhurst, CA. To my wonderful colleagues, friends and family, thank you for being yourselves and nurturing the many children that come into your lives. Special thanks to Karen Molenaar Terrell, author and educator from the Skagit Valley in WA and to Annie Barrett, artist, musician and educator from Bishop, CA for their inspired contributions to this collection. I appreciate the guidance and patience of the team at Xlibris as this project came to fruition.

Newborn

All fingers and toes
reaching,
reaching for the sky
extending, stretching
unfurling beyond

grasping, clasping
movement is a must

Two parents gaze enraptured
then stretch their arms
and touch,
touching
the new babe
reaching into their world

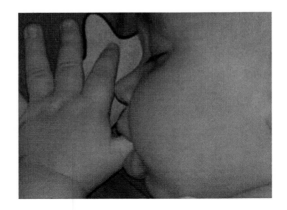

Trust

They brought you to me
after you were born
They lay you, crying, on my
shrinking belly and I sang you
a hymn and you stopped crying
and nuzzled my breast and I
looked on the top of your tiny wee
head and thought,
This is incredible

In The Night

To feel your warm head—
downy-soft with birth hair—
nestled under my chin
To wake and find your eyes
wide and studying my face—
innocent, guileless, pure
To feel you wriggling next to me
as you sleep
is unspeakable pleasure

Karen Molenaar Terrell

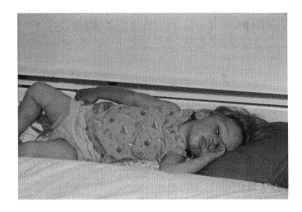

Sleeping Child

Restful now
>little angel
Brief calm
>vivacious one
Sweet face that melts the heart;
>Gentle twitch
>as dreams fleet by.

Are you climbing mountains?
>or sailing the deep, blue sea?
Perhaps you're fighting dragons
>or roaming a beach, wild & free.

O' special child
>little dreamer
Effervescence stilled for now;
>All of life's importance
nestled beneath your brow.

Daybreak

A drop of milk
spreads flat
on new oak table

Another drop joins as
they merge with morsel
of wheat next to
shiny white bowl painted
with blue flowers

A silver spoon clinks
on corelle then enters
rose bud lips

Plump hands wrap tightly
around handle
decorated with
floral geometrics . . .

an artist's rendering
a potter's craft
a farmer's grain
a cow's milk
a carpenter's skill

join in symphony
to feed this child
the days first meal

Northwest Child

(for Jeff)

Joyful scion
running barefoot
through dew-dappled grass

each green blade glistening
in a day that is also
drenched with sunshine

In the splash of dawns offering
moist creatures
jubilate

except for the few
whose viscous undersides
cling with fresh lawn clippings
and vine maple leaves
to the soles of
size three feet

And later, in the frog-filled
twilight
you and I scrape off
earthy collection
while the child sighs,
satisfied.

Moonlight and Shadows

Moonlight and shadows
in the night
whispers of awe and
secrets

Frogs chirping—
what
do they say?
Pondering their lingo
imaginations run away.

Musings pause as the moon's
full-orbed radiance
abruptly emerges,
crowning mountain,
silhouetting tree branches.
A five-year-old's slight fear
of night overtaken by wonder and light.

In the hush of beauty
the heavens beckon:
big dipper, pleiades,
Orion's belt . . .

Under glimmer and glow I linger
touched with peace and beauty,
filled with the inner joy,
the precious shared moments
of a moonlit night,
a chorus of frogs,
and a child

Pitter Patter

In the morn when I awake
I smile as I hear
little feet pitter patter.

Thoughts of problems unsolved
are chased away as
little feet pitter patter.

Could our worldly concerns
be solved in a minute
if we really listened
to the sound of little feet?

What a tonic it would be!
centering and calming,
little feet pitter patter
all around the world.

So, happily I await
snuggly warm softness;
little feet pitter patter,
vitalizing dawn.

My Favorite Time of Day

My favorite time of day
is when I first wake up
and run and jump in bed
with Mom and Dad—so snug!

My favorite time of day
is when I get to choose
what to have for breakfast—
pancakes, eggs or cheerios!

My favorite time of day
is when I go out to play
We run and jump; swing and slide;
fight pirates, dragons; chase butterflies!

Snuggling up with a bedtime book
is my favorite time of night;
Mom and Dad will read three or four—
sometimes . . . if I ask just right!

My most favorite time of night
is the way they tuck me in:
all cozy-warm with hugs and kisses
and the special things they say.

My favorite time of day
is when I go to sleep
and dream dreams . . . (yawn . . .)
of my favorite time of day.

But First, Can You Tie My Shoe?

I am going fishing, Mom
And I know just what to do,
Don't you worry, I'll be back later
But first, can you tie my shoe?

I'm going to fight off dinosaurs
There are lots of them coming for you.
Don't worry at all, by my sword they will fall
But first, can you pour me some juice?

I'm going to fly an airplane
Pilots know which way to look.
We'll fly up high and soar in the sky
But first, can you read me a book?

I'm going to ride my bike now
We'll be careful, don't fret about us.
I'll ride with my friend down to the road's end
But first, can you give me a push?

I am going to work now
Here's my lunch box, paper and glue.
See you later and have a nice day
But first, can you tie my shoe?

Precious Beginnings

Wasn't it just yesterday
you were but a lump
in my arms
cooing crazily
sucking toes
your big blue eyes
lighting up to see me?

How you entertained us
as you learned to walk
So, we never get to the movies
anymore—
we have an award-winning
toddler!

Then came three and four:
playgroups and preschool
exploring new venues
singing new songs;
discovery, delightful
discovery.

And now we're walking
to the bus stop.
Our five-year-old chattering
with excitement; his parents
vulnerable to this big change;
lumps in our throats.

But a child's bright eyes
are hard to resist.
We bravely smile
as you light up
at the sight of
the big yellow bus
which will carry you away
to a new world
of discovery.

First Day

Sailor dress
     clean and striped
tennis shoes
     new and white.

Hair that bounces
     baby-shampoo clean
Smile that glows
     big eyes that gleam.

Little arms that tightened
     in the best kind of hug
Waving goodbye
     to a heart that tugs.

The years have flown
     what can I say?
Our little girl
     started school today.

It Reminds Me

When I kneel
my little girl
runs to hug me.
She can reach my neck, my face.
"Mommy, I love you," she says.

It reminds me
to kneel more often
to pray
to be the right height
for a hug from an angel.

I tell my son
that I love him
as big
as the sky.
"Mommy," he says,
"I KNOW that."

It reminds me
that I must be doing
something right.

It reminds me
to keep
going.
It reminds me

Annie Barrett

Childhood Minutia

Outside: misty, cool dawn
quietness is broken by
waking birds and early commuters

Inside: bustling about
but not too harried
for talk over breakfast
of last night dreams . . .

Into the fog
we briskly walk
time for "hello!" to pony
and neighboring sheltie's
We jump up and down
to keep warm.

Then through the thick mist,
lights appear;
with a friendly roar
the school bus
arrives.

Sing to Me Again

I like to watch my daughter sleep,
stroke her cheek and brow
her peace is so complete
and drifts to me somehow.

Hush of dark pines near the window
Maybe just tomorrow
I'll wake before her,
Dress before the sun touches my old wood door.

Some evenings I feel like a dried up sponge
all the energy squeezed out
There's no more to give, no more to give
yet they demand it and a drop is wrung.

Squeeze a drop, squeeze a tear, my little one
Did I say I was at my end?
Fever at night, you call me to sing again
Your sheets are soaked with sweat.

But, who can argue with a snug warm body?
I've been battered and bruised
by infant heads
I've been strained and stretched by innocence.

Uterine strength
supersedes contraction
Did someone say this was fun?
Endless duty with stretch mark pay.

Have you ever argued with a nine-year-old?
Endless duty; gray hair pay.
Sometimes we break the cycle
Strong desire for harmony,
long moments of tears turns to
embracing relief.

I always knew I would have you, my children
Have you ever not been with me?
Thank you for my birthday cake made of sand
Delicious, decorated with cedar cones.

Please, sing to me again.
Sing to me again.

Annie Barrett and Jeannie O. Harsha

Holiday Fragrance

Christmas smells
evoke and entice
vibrant memories
of a carefree life . . .

Tobogganing down snow covered hills;
steaming cocoa to chase away chills
Snowball fights and round snowmen;
fresh-baked bread with homemade jam.

Advent candles in pungent fir wreath
dominate table laden with treats.
A crackling fire, we all gather round
with cinnamon cider as laughter abounds.

Secretly wrapping up gifts in red;
fresh whipped cream on gingerbread.
Caroling in the rousing crisp air;
a sense of wonder everywhere . . .

Memories beckon
through familiar scents;
Past and present bond
in loving fragrance.

January's Tree

Lonely now
in a quiet house
Your fragrance lingers

There's a browning beneath
needles shedding below
ornaments silent
hang without lighted glow

A week ago your lights shone
music filled the room
there was laughter; children
danced around you
inspecting colorful gifts

For nights we oohed and ahhed
as only tree lights lit the room
the angel in satin perched
at your crown

But I am not sad
on this silent, sweet-scented day
the angel is still there
happy memories gently touch
this quiet, peaceful day

Uncommon Frosting

'Twas the middle of February.
We'd given up on winter—
too warm but, oh well,
we played baseball instead
of sledding.

Then one morn . . .
I awoke with a start,
it was dark
and quiet.
"I think it snowed,"
came the deep, sleepy voice
beside me.

Joy! A dash to the window
confirmed it. The radio said
"buses running an hour late."
Joy again! The kids can sleep in.

Softly, down the stairs,
through a hushed house
I wander
from window to window,
charmed at the beauty
a fresh blanket brings . . .
A cover so rare
this near
the ocean.

Thumping, running . . .
What's going on?
I look up and behold
brother and sister child;
dashing from window to window,
young features awash with excitement.

"It snowed, it snowed!"
The happy cry hails in the morning
as we huddle before
the frosted pane.

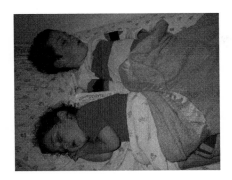

You two were sleeping . . .

. . . when I tiptoed into your room
last night
Soft sounds of breathing
a dreamer's duet.

The moon was waning
as I gazed at your still, small forms
who just an hour before
were teasing and laughing.

Sister child in somnio-nastics—
one knee in the air;
hair draped across pillow
like soft, dark silk.

Brother child's body
sprawled across bed;
head cradled in pillow
as I once cradled his infant self.

I watched you two sleeping
last night
and fell in love again

Head to Head at Sunrise

After evening storm
drove us into our tents,
we watched a rainbow grow

The vibrant patch expanded
and arched
right before our eyes!
The eyes of two mothers taking two
children on their first
backpack.

Sunsets after rainstorm
are most glorious!
We emerged from our tents,
spun around, eyes riveted upward,
dazzled
in all directions!

Later, cooking over camp stove
the lake below us reflected hues:
pink—orange—magenta.

Nighttime is sweet
tucked in our bags,
happily tired after a days
trek to high lakes, searching
for fish and finding
Autumn's peaceful beauty
among rocky ridges and delicate
leaves

Now dawn arrives with the soft
voice of a child,
"It's almost time, Mom!"

Still in our bags, we unzip
nylon screen
and, facing east,
head to head,
watch the soft morning light.

The Calm Before the Heat

On peaceful cool mornings
before summer sun arrives
I sip coffee and enjoy the quietude.

Dew drops cling
to lilacs and bare feet.
Bird song caresses
inner soul.
Hummers and bumble bees
search out nectar while
I search out strawberries
in the garden we share.
A lone cow moos . . .

The serenity of morning
prepares my way;
for when the sun bursts forth
and warms the land,
so then will my children
burst forth and warm
my heart.

Notes from a Little League Mom

My son was hot
in last night's game,
he hit two doubles
that nearly cleared the fence!

He got in a pickle, he did
but he's fast, full of fun
and has that special baseball sense;
he beat the pickle
with a head long dive and slide.

Second baseman fell on him in a steal attempt,
his elbow was ground into the dirt
but the ball was lost and my son,
he headed for third.

He sailed for home when the next batter hit,
put some ice on his elbow for 10 seconds,
just a thought, then donned the catchers gear
for the field once again.

He trapped those wild pitches,
threw a bunter out at first,
tagged a stealer at home plate . . .

You know, he's so skinny! .
his strong arm and quick-thinking response
astound me at times.

This may sound like a brag but, really
I'm just reciting a tale from one of
those times when I've been hit
with the insight of a child's growth in skills,
been caught with the detail that he's
grown in sense,
and felt grounded in the knowledge
of his growth in teamwork.

As these facts slide into home base,
I feel the triumph of runs scored
for us all.

Play Right

We played basketball last night.
One of those rare games where
competition was balanced with respect.
Little players were passed to and
their confidence grew.
Big players didn't lose sight
of the joy of the game
no competitive blurring of vision.

Sometimes we do things just right.
We played basketball last night.
We played it right.

First Day, New School

They couldn't sleep the night before
new clothes laid out
sneakers shined
anticipation riding high

The morning rush
was pressed with simmering
excitement
a little trepidation mixed in:
a blend—new school but some familiar friends

6th grade boy jumps out
rushes off
"come to my class some other day mom—
like when you're volunteering."

4th grade daughter
takes my hand;
together we walk
to new classroom
new teacher; new
and old friends

The bell rings
she finds her seat;
busy now
but as she looks up;
I blow her a kiss

and slip
out the door

In This Moment

Blue flowers and green
form the pattern of her coverlet.
Hugging her young body,
my head on her shoulder,
vision is flooded by floral blues and greens.

Six days without her is a long time for me . . .
My heart feels warm
to have her back.
But my mind is seeking clarity;
Sorting through strong emotions
to the one truth—
she is a beloved child
This sickness will not hinder her.

We are quiet together
Calm, strong thoughts pass between us
Tender and strong
In this moment of my life.

There are times to be joyful
There are times to be sad
There are times to be playful
and times to be serious.

This is a serious time
Serious about the truth of things
Not time to worry and fret
Time to be strong, time to be tender
time to see clearly
In this moment of my life.

I think of how we rush
through the days
barely aware of the most important things
so I become aware of this moment
aware of this child
aware of this relationship so unique
In this moment in my life.

Badger Pass — Gliding Into a New Year

Soft snow
beneath our skis
makes turning easy as slicing
pumpkin pie.

Your red cheeks hide
freckles and enhance
the excitement
in your eyes as you tell
me of skiing your first black
diamond.

At eleven years old,
I love you
and relish this parent-child
New Year's day.
I ask a friendly snow boarder
to capture us together,
handing her my camera
as you glide in beside me

on the snowy slope that we later
r
  a
    c
     e   d
          o
            w
              n
together,
s w o o s h i n g
past other happy skiers
and into
cool, sweet memories

for life.

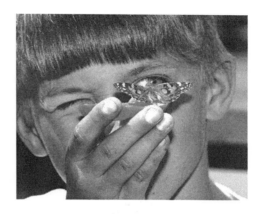

Reminder

Rushing off to work
and school, the child points out
a butterfly

Nine Years Old

She does her own pony tail now;
it swings
with independence

Evening

Dancing on the deck
her rhythm leads me
as the sky turns
purple

Untitled

At eleven he defies
and questions me
in every way

*but that night in the tent
when the wind was howling . . .*

Each day brings something of a challenge
the lack of thought preceding action
the slow movement to parental commands

*but that night in the tent
when the wind was howling . . .*

He demands more rights,
teases his sister to hysterics,
catches me at each lame excuse

Yet . . . we are growing, maturing together
our paths converge
along the bumpy road

And each time I feel stretched beyond reason
I remember

that night in the tent
when the wind was howling
he snuggled close, called me "mommy" instead of "Maa-om . . ."
and felt safe.

Fledgling

Here you are, at the close of the elementary years—
somewhere between fledgling and woman

Boys are still strange creatures—of little interest to you
Girls are full of fun and giggles!

I watch you with a full heart
You, who are so loving
You'd adopt a homeless person
Rescue all the abandoned cats in the world
Save the lame dogs you've seen on our trips to Mexico

My heart is brimming as I watch you dance
Making up routines to many beats
making your brother and dad laugh or
roll their eyes; you are a spark
of energy and life,
itself.

But, I feel you're on the brink of change
heading off to middle school
your body changing
a little girl no more . . .

Other adults warn me about adolescence
and it's many vicissitudes;
why should I fear change
why should I fear our close relationship
will pale?

We've come far already, you and I
We come through change everyday
I will only expect progress
I will only expect betterment.

For you have given me so much already
Why should anything be taken away?
You are a gift that keeps getting better

I am here to help you fly.

Remember—Now

I glance at old pictures
cute, chubby toddlers
growing into skinny kids
so small, so sweet, so pliable . . .

the memories flow in—
lots of hugs, tears easily
wiped away; chatty talks on the way home
from school or games.

Things have changed . . .
now they look like adults—almost
yet they are not
Moods change as often as birds appear
in Spring
The way home is often quiet; sometimes sulky.
Arguments transport me
back to my teenage-hood
sometimes I forget
to be the parent

Yet it struck me one day, the need
is still the same:
to feel special; to be honored; to have someone
excited to see them at the end of their day;
the need for unconditional love

So I try to listen, without distraction, when they talk
I try to react unemotionally when they
are emotional; I don't
always succeed

Yet I know the striving is important
to be the parent is important
this time in their life will never occur again and I want to touch
them gently, yet firmly
let them know they are loved
lift them up, let them fly on
into adulthood
supported by an honoring love

Weeding

My son and I weeded the garden today
we talked of corn plants and tomatoes
then of weeds, roots and water and sun
plants grow and we grow

Then he told me his desires
and things he thought unfair
I thinned out corn and listened

Ye have ears but do ye hear?

I gave advice but he stuck to his guns

My heart had compassion for him
we pollinated tomatoes and watered the lot

we're still growing and the sun is now high

As Time Goes by

There you are—
tall now
discerning our wry humor;
not taking us seriously
unless your allowance is threatened . . .

What happened to my chubby, little child
who, just yesterday ran into my arms—
your mother, #1 in your life?
Now, you ask your friends for advice . . .

Yet, your antics amuse me still,
Goofy young teen; all arm and leg energy;
with growing awareness of all life's treasures-
friends, ball games; good teachers and grandparents.

I learn so much from you
as time goes by.
The obvious, like patience and humility
The not-so-obvious like focused listening;
how to keep my humor after 5p.m.; how to not yell
when you're late for the umpteenth time; how to balance
being parent and friend.

For you need both, as I do.
We'll trade roles on and off I suspect;
as time goes by . . .

And I'll continue to watch the show—
you—growing in wisdom and stature
and grace; my cherished child.

To My 15-year-old

Hey, big boy
you sure have grown
from chubby babe to skinny
kid and, now, wow—a handsome dude!

The way we argue isn't so bad
I guess,
Once we learn to respect each
other and get the understanding straight

You're a thinker
that's good;
a reasoner,
hard on parents but sets us thinking, too

I reflect on all the years so far,
the struggles the laughter
the tears, the heart wrenching times
and the pride that I have for you
My big, handsome, energetic, thoughtful,
thinking, caring, lanky 15-year-old.

Layers

Shrek talked about layers,
like an onion.
That's you, dear.
You have so many interesting
layers.
Some subtly hidden
but simmering underneath the surface.

The beautiful surface that is made
more so by the big heart
beneath.

Soul child—so full
of life and layers of
craziness, compassion.
You're mischievous and caring;
Somethimes a sparkler
sometimes a single candle
casting a gentle radiance
in the darkness.

You will light the way for many;
Your life will be a joyful scrimmage.
Your faith and love, compassion and determination . . .
All the layers . . . will lead you
as your light guides the way.

Wistful Love

Here we are at the brink of change—
Our daughter's senior year

College catalogs are pored over
Orientation invitations pour in
The Navy wants her, too

We   want   her
To find the right fit
To soar and be happy
to   learn   discern   grow

We hold back when It doesn't feel right
Exploring whether it's personal
or real
this bittersweet time for parents

We work hard to bury wistfulness
as deep as we can and go with her energy
ride her enthusiasm
guide her with experience

For we ARE here
to help her fly

Get Published, Inc!
Thorofare, NJ 08086
05 February, 2010
BA2010036